Piano · Vocal · Guitar

# twentysomething jamie cullum

ISBN 0-634-08372-4

HAL•LEONARD®
CORPORATION

7777 W. BLUEMOUND RD. P.O. BOX 13819 MILWAUKEE, WI 53213

Visit Hal Leonard Online at
**www.halleonard.com**

# THESE ARE THE DAYS

Words and Music by
BEN CULLUM

# TWENTYSOMETHING

Words and Music by
JAMIE CULLUM

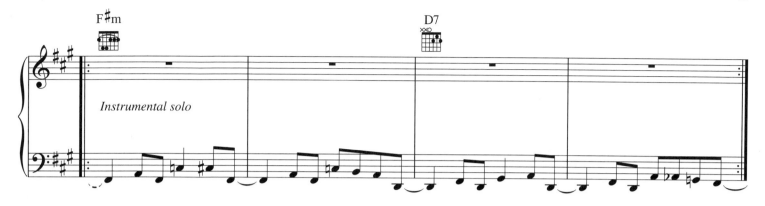

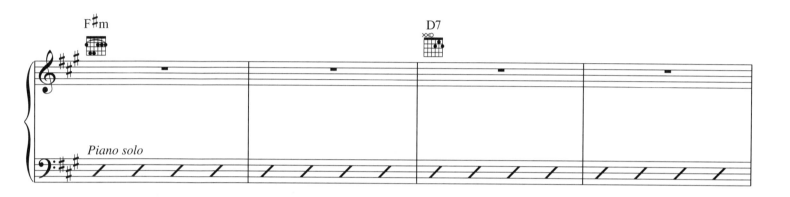

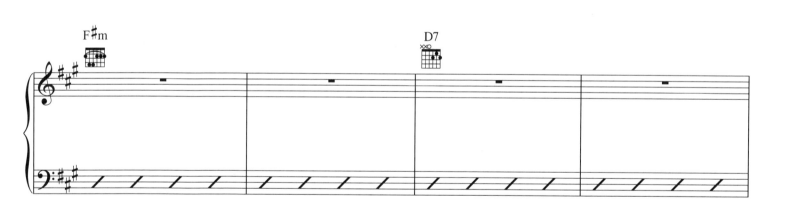

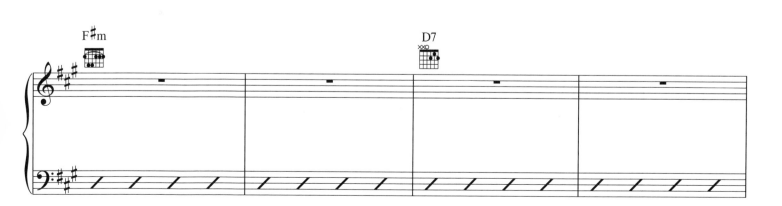

# THE WIND CRIES MARY

Words and Music by
JIMI HENDRIX

Af-ter all ___ the jacks ___ are in their box-es

and the clowns have all ___ gone to bed,

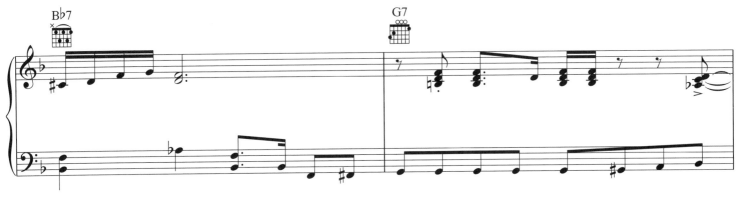

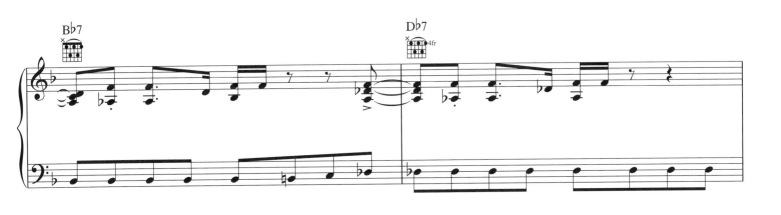

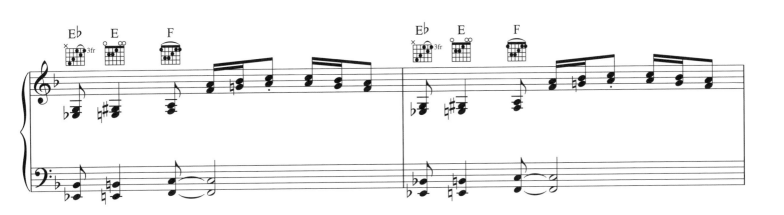

# ALL AT SEA

Words and Music by
JAMIE CULLUM

# LOVER, YOU SHOULD'VE COME OVER

Words and Music by
JEFF BUCKLEY

# SINGIN' IN THE RAIN

Lyric by ARTHUR FREED
Music by NACIO HERB BROWN

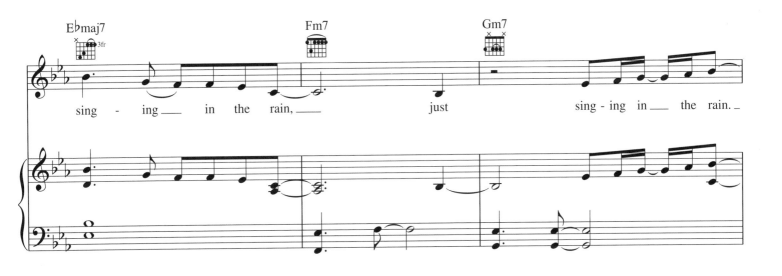

(1st time only) in the rain,

in the rain.

Da ba do___ do do do do do da do.___

**Repeat and Fade**

Da ba do___ do do do do do da do.___

# I GET A KICK OUT OF YOU
## from ANYTHING GOES

Words and Music by
COLE PORTER

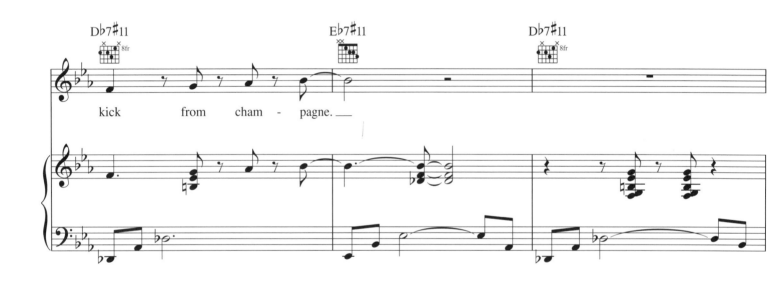

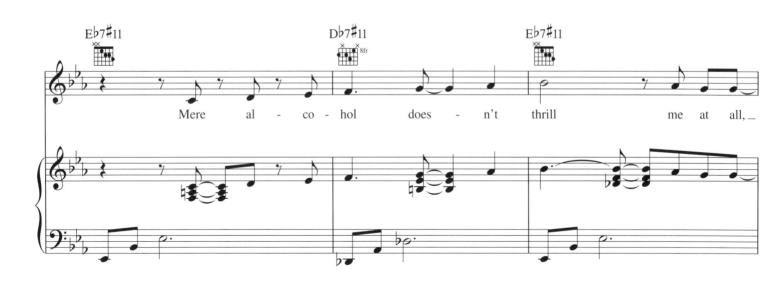

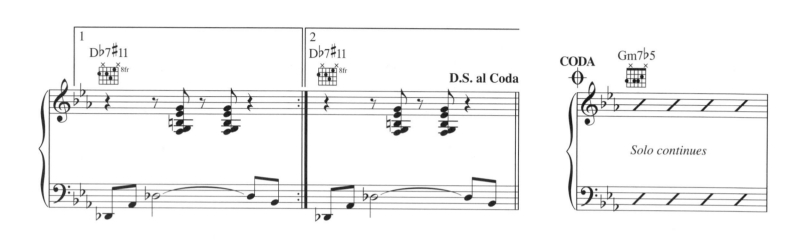

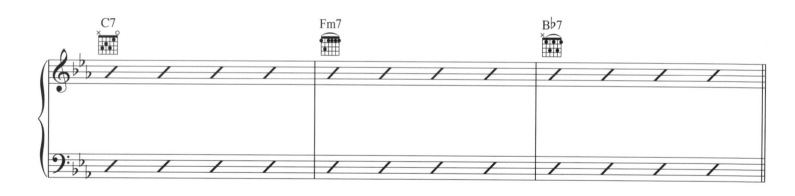

# BLAME IT ON MY YOUTH

Words by EDWARD HEYMAN
Music by OSCAR LEVANT

**Slowly**

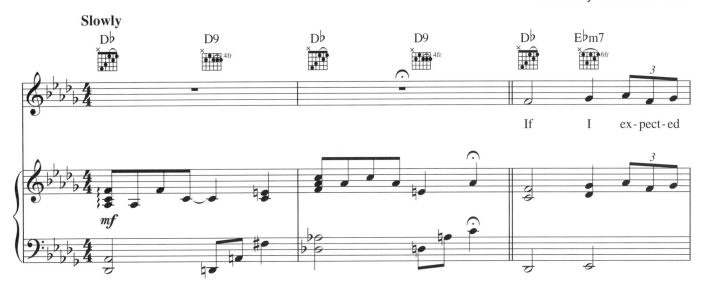

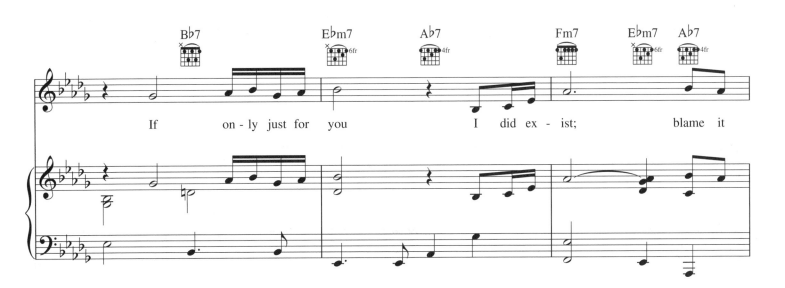

# HIGH AND DRY

Words and Music by THOMAS YORKE,
EDWARD O'BRIEN, COLIN GREENWOOD,
JONATHAN GREENWOOD and PHILIP SELWAY

# IT'S ABOUT TIME

Words and Music by
BEN CULLUM

Moderately, with a beat

Walk-ing down_ to the wa-ter's edge_ where I have been be-fore,_ if
Try too hard_ and it feels just like_ you're run-ning on_ thin air._

I don't find_ my love_ some-time_ I'm walk-ing out_ that door._ The
Why does love hap-pen by_ sur-prise_ if you don't real-ly care?_

Some may come_ and some may go,_ but no one seems_ to be_____ the
past is gone,_ the flames_ are out_ from fires_ that_ have burned._

# BUT FOR NOW

Words and Music by
BOB DOROUGH

But for

# I COULD HAVE DANCED ALL NIGHT

from MY FAIR LADY

Words by ALAN JAY LERNER
Music by FREDERICK LOEWE

**Funk beat**

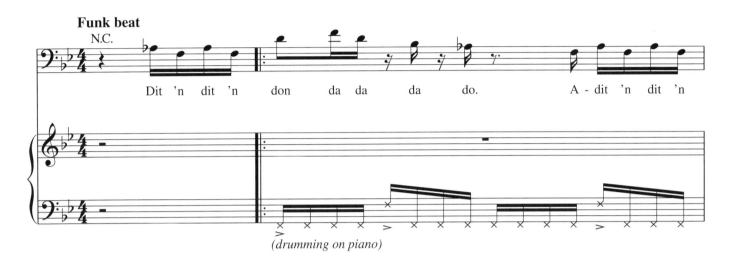

(drumming on piano)

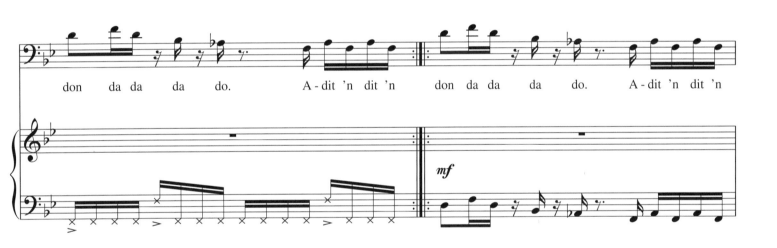

danced          all                    night.

Bed, _____        I could-n't    go

to  bed.          My  head's too light  to  try  and  set - tle down. _

Sle -        ep,              I could-n't    sleep

D.S. al Coda

to - night, __ not for all the jewels in the crown. ___

**CODA**

N.C.

when she ___ be-gan to dance with __ me, __

Gb13    F7

__ I could have danced, danced, __ danced. ___

Amaj7b5    Em7b5    Bbm(maj7)    Bm(maj7)

# NEXT YEAR, BABY

Words and Music by
JAMIE CULLUM

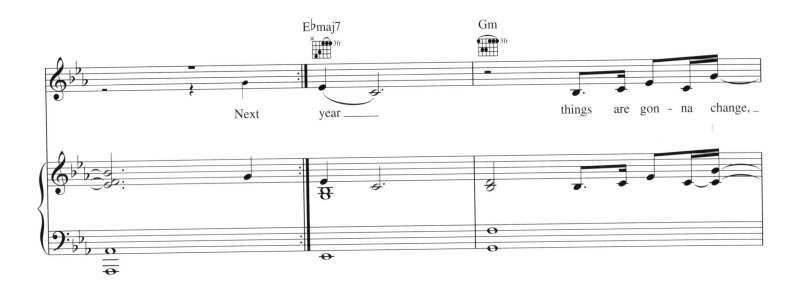

# WHAT A DIFF'RENCE A DAY MADE

English Words by STANLEY ADAMS
Music and Spanish Words by MARIA GREVER

C000003753

# Take another ten

piano

arranged by Mike Cornick

www.universaledition.com
vienna · london · new york

UE 21 171

ISMN: M-008-06753-2
UPC 8-03452-01611-3
ISBN 978-3-7024-1895-4

# Preface

*Take Another 10* offers a new selection of piano arrangements of pieces which range in style from the 16th Century English air *Greensleeves* to the 20<sup>th</sup> Century 'classic pop' *Your Song* by Elton John.

Apart from *Espagnol*, an original composition which is published here for the first time, one common factor clearly links this very diverse collection, and that is the well-established popularity of each of the pieces. Even the song, *Moscow Nights*, which may be less well known outside Russia, proved to be very popular in the U.K. in the 1960's in the form of a traditional jazz arrangement under the title *Midnight in Moscow*.

All of the arrangements in this selection have been written specifically for inclusion in this volume.

# Vorwort

*Take Another 10* ist eine neue Sammlung von Klavierbearbeitungen von Stücken, die stilistisch vom englischen Air *Greensleeves* aus dem 16. Jahrhundert bis zum „klassischen Popsong" von Elton John *Your Song* aus dem 20. Jahrhundert reichen.

Außer *Espagnol*, einer eigenständigen, hier zum ersten Mal veröffentlichten Komposition, vereint offensichtlich ein Umstand diese unterschiedlichen Beiträge, und das ist die weit verbreitete Beliebtheit jedes dieser Stücke. Selbst das Lied, *Moscow Nights*, das man vielleicht außerhalb Russlands weniger kennt, erfreute sich in Großbritannien in den 1960er Jahren großer Beliebtheit in Form eines traditionellen Jazzarrangements unter dem Titel *Midnight in Moscow*.

Alle in dieser Sammlung erscheinenden Bearbeitungen wurden speziell für diesen Band geschrieben.

# Préface

*Take Another 10* propose une nouvelle sélection d'arrangements pour piano de pièces dont les styles s'étendent de l'air anglais du XVIe siècle *Greesleeves* à la chanson 'pop classique' *Your Song* d'Elton John.

A l'exception d'*Espagnol*, composition originale publiée ici pour la première fois, un point commun relie directement les pièces formant ce recueil très varié, à savoir la très grande célébrité de chacune d'elles. Même la chanson *Moscow Nights*, sans doute peu connue en dehors de la Russie, a connu un grande popularité en Grande-Bretagne dans les années 1960, sous la forme d'un arrangement traditionnel de jazz intitulé *Midnight in Moscow*.

Tous les arrangements de cette sélection ont été spécialement réalisés en vue de constituer ce volume.

*Mike Cornick*

# Contents

# Acknowledgements

I would like to thank Bill Lee and Daria Gromyko for the loan of Russian publications of *Moscow Nights* and Bill Lee and Kate Willmott for their appreciative comments and for playing through some of these arrangements.

# Air
## from Orchestral Suite No.3 in D [BWV 1068]

Johann Sebastian Bach
(1685–1750)
Arr. Mike Cornick

**Lento cantabile** ♩ = 35

UE 21 171

4

# Greensleeves
## (1580 or earlier)

Traditional
Arr. Mike Cornick

UE 21 171

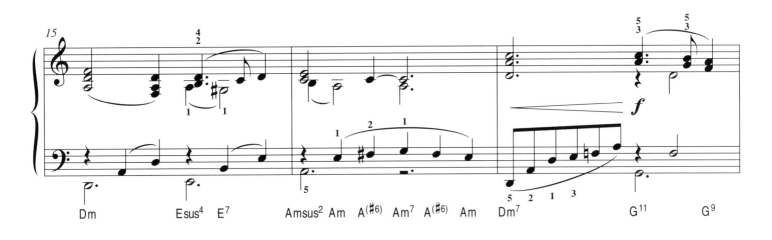

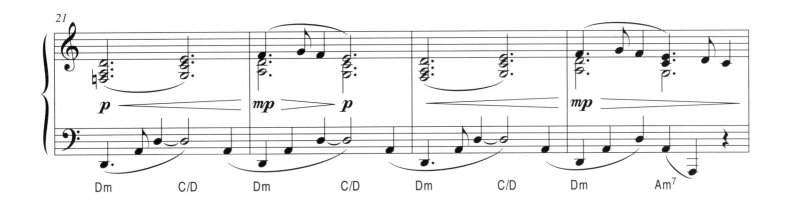

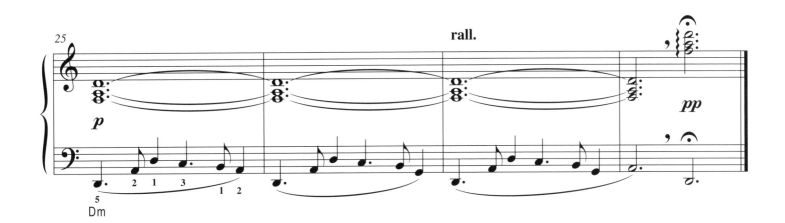

# Ave Verum Corpus
## Motet KV 618

Wolfgang Amadeus Mozart
(1756-1791)
Arr. Mike Cornick

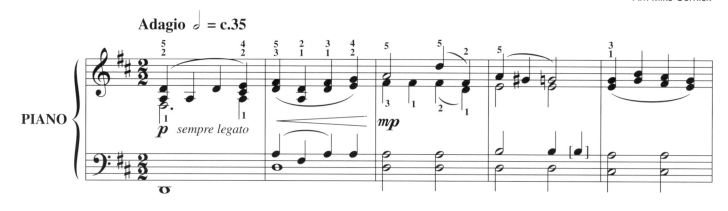

\* The cue-size notes represent purely instrumental decoration and should be played
quieter than the main melody for choir below.

UE 21 171

# Your Song

Words and Music by
Elton John & Bernie Taupin
Arr. Mike Cornick

UE 21 171

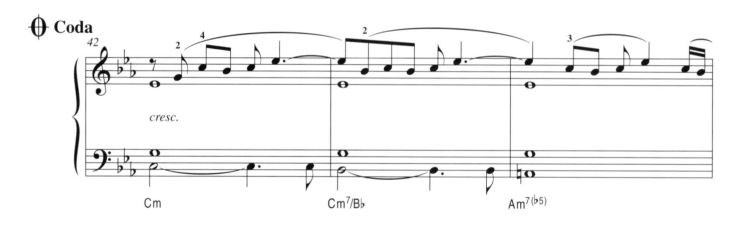

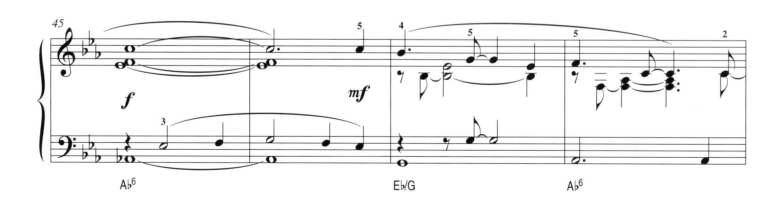

# Londonderry Air
## first published in 1855

Traditional Irish Air
Arr. Mike Cornick

UE 21 171

# Espagnol

Mike Cornick
(1947)

**PIANO**

UE 21 171

# Moscow Nights

Vasily Solovev-Sedoj
(1907–1979)
Arr. Mike Cornick

UE 21 171

# Evening Prayer
## from the opera *Hansel and Gretel*

Engelbert Humperdinck
(1854-1921)
Arr. Mike Cornick

UE 21 171

# Swing Low

American Traditional
Arr. Mike Cornick

UE 21 171

# When I Fall In Love

Words by Edward Heyman
Music by Victor Young
Arr. Mike Cornick

UE 21 171